DIY Woodwork:

Beginner's Guide How to Build a Sauna

Disclaimer: All photos used in this book, including the cover photo were made available under a <u>Attribution-ShareAlike 2.0 Generic (CC BY-SA 2.0)</u> and sourced from <u>Flickr</u>

Copyright 2016 by Publisher – All rights reserved.

This document is geared towards providing exact and reliable information in regards to the topic and issue covered. The publication is sold with the idea that the publisher is not required to render accounting, officially permitted, or otherwise, qualified services. If advice is necessary, legal or professional, a practiced individual in the profession should be ordered.

- From a Declaration of Principles which was accepted and approved equally by a Committee of the American Bar Association and a Committee of Publishers and Associations.

In no way is it legal to reproduce, duplicate, or transmit any part of this document in either electronic means or in printed format. Recording of this publication is strictly prohibited and any storage of this document is not allowed unless with written permission from the publisher. All rights reserved.

The information provided herein is stated to be truthful and consistent, in that any liability, in terms of inattention or otherwise, by any usage or abuse of any policies, processes, or directions contained within is the solitary and utter responsibility of the recipient reader. Under no circumstances will any legal responsibility or blame be held against the publisher for any reparation, damages, or monetary loss due to the information herein, either directly or indirectly.

Respective authors own all copyrights not held by the publisher.

The information herein is offered for informational purposes solely, and is universal as so. The presentation of the information is without contract or any type of guarantee assurance.

The trademarks that are used are without any consent, and the publication of the trademark is without permission or backing by the trademark owner. All trademarks and brands within this book are for clarifying purposes only and are the owned by the owners themselves, not affiliated with this document.

Table of Contents

DIY Woodwork: 1
Beginner's Guide How to Build a Sauna..1
Introduction: Just what exactly is a Sauna?...4
Chapter 1: Building Your Own Sauna 6
    Clear and Prep your Workspace 6
    Constructing Your Walls..8
    Install Your Sauna Heater 9
    Add Your Rocks to Your Heater 10
    Setting up Your Benches..11
    Install Ventilation System..11
Chapter 2: The Potential Benefits and Detriments of using a Sauna..................13
    The Treatment of Rheumatoid Arthritis..13
    Impact of Sauna on Breathing 14
    Sauna and Hormones 15
    Sauna and the Cardiovascular System...15
    Losing Weight through Sauna Exposure 16
    Sauna and Alcohol...17
Chapter 3: Alternative Sauna Designs 19
    Bathroom Sauna 19
    The Porta Potty Sauna 21
    Turn Your Shed into a Sauna 22
    The Public Telephone Booth Sauna...23
    From Beater Van to Awesome Sauna..24
    Turn your Closet into a Sauna 25
Conclusion: Feeling the heat!..26

Introduction: Just what exactly is a Sauna?

At its most basic level a sauna can be said to be simply any space that has been created to handle high heat and humidity for the purpose of allowing people to sit inside of it to experience the environment. The first known saunas were found in the northern reaches of Finland in which early sauna enthusiasts dug up pits in the ground and employed heated stones to bring heat to their participants. In fact the word "sauna" comes from Finnish, which translates roughly in English as "bathhouse".

The sauna typically used a fireplace to heat up masonry in order to produce the heat needed for the sauna. Sauna users would then pour water on these hot pieces of masonry so that steam would rise up and expose those around it to their heat. These saunas were very refreshing for those who used them during Finland's ice cold winters.

These ancient saunas would then eventually transform into the modern saunas that we see today, which host a wide variety of technical capacity. Saunas today are also used for a wide variety of purposes. They can be utilized to detox the body, help induce fat burn, increase energy, and even to improve cosmetic features of the body such as adding thickness to hair and enhancing elasticity of the skin. However you use a sauna, you can be sure that it will greatly benefit and improve your life.

I can still remember the first time I used a sauna, and it was nothing short of a life changing experience. Me and some friends of mine were on a backpacking tour of Greece when we ran into what constituted a local sauna for Athens. Basically a bunch of dudes hanging out in a steam drenched room.

It may not sound too appealing to an untrained imagination, but after just a few minutes I could feel the difference! I could breathe better and was much more relaxed. I remember asking my friend at the time, "Is this what a sauna is?" In which he quickly replied, "Yes my friend—yes it is."

Chapter 1: Building Your Own Sauna

There are a few ways to build a sauna, depending on type, and just what you want to get out of it. Primarily, you could build a classic dry sauna just like the Finnish used, in which the internal temps hover around 80 degrees, or you could build a wet sauna, that holds the same temperature but with much greater humidity. The higher humidity level is helpful to facilitate easier breathing in the heat.

If you have allergies or asthma you are going to want to build a sauna with a bit of humidity. I know from my own personal experience suffering with asthma, that the second I step into a dry sauna, I feel the air being sucked right out of my lungs like I'm suffocating (not a pleasant experience). A wet sauna on the other hand is much more conducive to the asthmatic and allergy prone such as myself, so to be on the safe side, let's put our money on the wet sauna!

But first let's go over some basics! In this chapter we are going to give you the rundown of how you can build your own Sauna using material you can find practically just laying around the house. You don't need much money, and you don't even need much effort. If you are simply armed with an attention to detail, you have more than what you need to get the job done.

Clear and Prep your Workspace

Whether you are installing your sauna in the garage or the backyard, you need to make sure that you have ample space to work in. I would recommend taking out anything that will not be of use to you and send it off to be recycled. After all, just because you can't use it, doesn't mean that someone else can't! Along with junk items you need to also remove any drywall that may be present since this material is not conducive to the heat and humidity of a sauna.

Drywall would actually cause excessive mold and would essential spell the end of our sauna. So get rid of your drywall. For much the same reason as why you got rid of your drywall, you also need to have a non-permeable floor, meaning a floor that moisture can not penetrate. Cement floors are perfect for this, but so are tile and vinyl floors.

So if your floor isn't already non permeable you will need to make it that way by either laying down tile, vinyl, or cement covering. Once your area is clear and prepped, you should then sketch out a basic diagram of the space that you are using. You don't have to have graduated from engineering school for this one, just a basic schematic will do. Just as long as you sketch out the room and your source of heat, this will be your blueprint when you begin construction.

Once you decide upon where you want to take your design, stick with it. There is no reason for you to deviate from your initial set of plans. So until the day of your build, make sure you keep these plans in a safe place. I know that you are doing this out of the comfort of your own home. But nevertheless, no matter where the job is, if you want it to be professionally done, you have to act like nothing less than a professional!

Constructing Your Walls

It goes without saying that if you would like to maintain heat inside a sauna then you will need to install some insulation. Take some R-11 insulation and apply it to your interior walls. After your walls are insulated you will want to create what is known as a "moisture barrier". This moisture barrier is a special layer designed to further insulate the walls from accumulating extra moisture from the steam and heat that they will be constantly exposed to.

This moisture barrier can be constructed from common aluminum foil found in any household kitchen drawer. Just spread this foil out and slap it right over your layer of insulation. You can hold this material in place with just some basic masking tape. After your moisture barrier and insulation are in place, you will then want to install your cedar paneling directly over these two layers. Start off in the top right corner of the room, and place your first boards up on the wall in that corner.

From this starting place the rest of the boards, one after the other, end to end until an entire row of cedar wood paneling is covering that section of the wall. When this row is completed, immediately create another row right underneath and repeat the pattern. Continue this process until the entire wall is covered, if you run into a light switch, simply cut your wood to where you can go around it as needed. Nail these boards in place over your insulation

Install Your Sauna Heater

One of the best heaters that you could use for this project is one called a "Polar HMR 60". These heaters come with a set of screws to latch the unit to the wall; two of the screws are longer than the others. It is these screws that will be used to hold the top of the unit to the wall. The screws may not seem that strong, but they are a lot stronger than they look, and as soon as you hook the heater up to the wall with them, it will be stuck on their pretty good.

You should mark on the wall exactly where you would like to place these screws ahead of time. Now screw in the top screws just as specified, and follow this up by screwing in the bottom screws as well. After this you will need to install a guard rail or some other barrier around the heating unit just to make sure that no one accidentally trips and falls on it.

A feat that is rather easy to do! I can't tell you how many times that I myself almost fell face first right into the heater! That's what the safety rails are for though, to prevent us from succumbing to our own fumbling and bumbling! If you are accident prone like me, definitely install these rails!

Add Your Rocks to Your Heater

As a rule, you should always wash your sauna heater rocks prior to putting them inside the unit. This will get rid of any dirt or debris on your rocks, helping to prevent any unpleasant odors emanating from your heater. When putting your rocks in your heating unit, place them behind the element so that the sensors inside the unit do not get falsely activated. These stone heating rocks have been used for thousands of years to keep saunas warm. And you will not be disappointed with their use today either! The key is just to maintain them so that they give off the best heat they can muster for as long as they can!

Setting up Your Benches

Now that the main components of what makes your sauna, a *sauna*, are in place, you will want to set up your benches, so that you and your guests will have somewhere to rest while they soak up the warmth of the room. Typically in this you would create a high bench and a low one, with the low bench twice as wide as the high one, reaching all the way to the wall.

The typical bench is also about 18 inches deep, and will need 2 x 2 supports in order to stay afloat. You might also want to add some lighting underneath for aesthetic effect. I put some small headlamps underneath mine so that I could lay down and read while I was in the sauna. Just one word of caution on this one—if you read in the sauna—you *will* fall asleep!

Install Ventilation System

The first thing you should look out for—and it goes right along with what we just mentioned about asthma and breathing—is proper ventilation. In order to have a decent air supply in your sauna and avoid suffocation, you have to have properly circulated air vented into the building. This is the airflow that will keep you happy in your sauna, so be sure to install it.

In order to do this you need to place (or already have) what is known as an upper outlet vent a few inches off the ground, in order to facilitate air flow. With yet another vent placed right by the source of your sauna's heat itself. These vents are important so that excessive eat can have a place in which to exit. The air needs to be able to be guided in and then guided back out. Please make sure you get this right, its very important.

Chapter 2: The Potential Benefits and Detriments of using a Sauna

Everything in life has its positives and negatives, and the same can be said for the use of saunas. There are many health benefits that can be derived from the practice but there are some possible risks and detriments that you should be aware of as well. In this chapter we will explore them all.

The Treatment of Rheumatoid Arthritis

Many have sung the praises of how saunas can benefit those who are afflicted with all kinds of rheumatoid arthritis; but does it really work? So far, the answer to this question is fairly positive. And recent studies have in fact indicated that in general, routine immersion in the heat of saunas does in fact improve the mobility of joints, and relieve much of the pain associated with arthritis.

But still others have indicated that despite the initial soothing feeling that a sauna can bring, shortly afterwards the pain often returns even worse once out of the sauna. So whether or not saunas are truly effective in the treatment of Rheumatoid Arthritis largely seems to dependant on who you talk to. More research still needs to be done, but if nothing else is working for you. It certainly wouldn't hurt you to give this special treatment a try.

Impact of Sauna on Breathing

We all need to breathe right? Unfortunately the heat of a sauna can sometimes make breathing more difficult. I know this first hand as an asthma suffers—and there were times—that I have walked into saunas and felt the air ripped right out of my lungs. Its not a good feeling, and if this happens to you, it may discourage you from participating in sauna use in the future. Scientifically speaking the heat of a sauna will decrease your pulmonary congestion, while simultaneously increases the total expiratory volume of your lungs.

In other words; you can't breathe! Obviously this isn't always the case, or no one would use a sauna. But on rare occasions and for a certain few with acute asthma and allergy symptoms, the impact a sauna can have on your breathing are quite detrimental. These affects can be mitigated, but they have to be given a chance. So just make sure you know the impact that the sauna has on our lungs and our breathing.

Sauna and Hormones

Regular trips to the sauna have been known to help regulate hormones. And there has been much debate about this, but there does seem to be a connection between raising core body temperature through the use of a sauna and the regulation of hormones. It can't be denied that those with hormone imbalances do feel different upon entry into a sauna.

In particular, sauna exposure triggers the sympathetic nervous system, lowering stress hormones such as cortisol. With cortisol kept in check, insulin, thyroid, estrogen, and testosterone are able to regain their balance. Exposure to saunas also aids in the increase of adrenal secretions of adolsterone, helping to regulate our electrolytes in the process.

Sauna and the Cardiovascular System

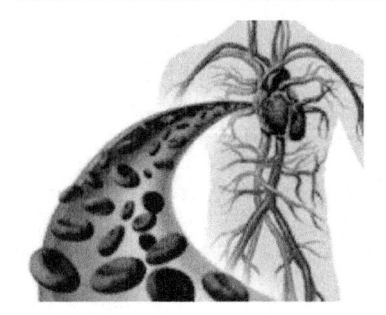

Inside the confines of a warm sauna, our core temperature rises, causing dilation of the blood vessels in your body. This then—of course—leads to increased blood circulation throughout your entire body. This of course is a very good thing for your health, and should be sought after any chance you get.

This increased blood flow will then improve the distribution of oxygen throughout the entire cardiovascular system. And right along with this improved circulation and oxygenation, just being in the environment of a sauna itself aids in improving overall the output of the heart itself. Without even having to exercise, the atmosphere of the sauna is working your heart for you!

This is actually an ideal condition and therapy for those who are bound in wheelchairs or otherwise can't walk and move around that well. By just stepping into a sauna, they can have their heart work a little bit harder to keep up with the heat, helping them stay a little bit healthier in the long run as well.

Losing Weight through Sauna Exposure

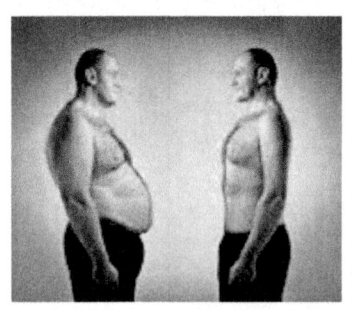

It has long been believed that sweating it out in the sauna can help in weight loss. There is truth to this due to the simple fact that saunas increase the heart rate while simultaneously lowering blood pressure; thereby increasing metabolism and leading to weight loss. Some sauna participants have been known to burn as much as 600 calories for every 30 minutes they spent in the sauna! If you are trying to lose weight this is certainly nothing to sneeze at!

Sauna and Alcohol

Drinking alcohol while in the Sauna can pose some serious problems for your health. The risk you run in particular is succumbing to hypotension. The complete opposite of *hypertension,* hypotension is the condition of having dangerously low blood pressure. While in the heat of the sauna, the more you drink, the lower your blood pressure gets, the lower your blood pressure gets the more likely you will pass out.

Quite easily put; alcohol and sauna's are a recipe for disaster. When in a sauna you need to be cognitively alert enough to monitor your own condition, but alcohol takes away from that. The more you drink, the less acutely you become aware of your surroundings and the greater your risk of drinking yourself into a low blood pressure stupor, sprawled out on the bench or floor of your sauna!

Alcohol also increases the risk of arrhythmias and heart attacks when used excessively before or during sauna treatments. I hate to be a bummer here, but its important, and you should probably save your alcoholic beverages for *after* you get *out* of the sauna!

Chapter 3: Alternative Sauna Designs

Now that we have discussed conventional sauna design and its benefits, let's take a look at some of the more *unconventional* designs that can be used. The examples depicted here range from the slightly different to the downright bizarre. Check out these alternative sauna designs in all their strange splendor and ridiculousness!

Bathroom Sauna

If you think about it, the bathroom makes for the perfect place to build a sauna. It's already water proof, and already used to humidity from hot water, it's just the technical aspects of the transformation that might seem daunting or somewhat strange to those who hear it. The construction of a bathroom sauna may seem far fetched to some, but with just some intelligent tweaks of your bathroom structure, you can find yourself cutting what your sauna cost would otherwise be, in half.

With a bathroom sauna just two standard heaters should do the trick. One of the keys of installing a sauna in your bathroom is to make sure that all of the fittings and fixtures are stable and not prone to warping in the heat of the sauna. Remember the damaging power of heat and water, and always do your best to guard against it. Once you have done this, the next thing that you will need to do is make sure that you insulate your bathroom with some good cotton based insulation.

Cotton insulation is cheap to buy and easy to install. After installing your insulation, you can place a vapor barrier on the walls to enhance the steam of the sauna. Post it up on your bathroom wall with tape to cover the seams of your bathroom. There shouldn't be any cracks or crevices exposed. Even places you have nailed into your wooden materials (as we will get into next) should be sealed off to prevent exposure.

Bathroom sauna construction is comprised primarily of cedar wood since cedar wood does not contract or expand when subjected to heat. It also provides good insulation, making it unlikely to become rotted out. There are 7 categories of cedar wood, but the best for this task will undoubtedly be proprietary grade cedar wood. This way you will know that your wood is of a quality degree and has been treated against mold and insect infestation.

Because believe me, there is nothing worse than constructing a sauna only to breathe in a steady stream of nasty mold! So get your wood varnished and treated! Next, create the bench that you and your guests will sit on for your bathroom sauna. It doesn't have to be fancy; in fact the old wooden frame of a couch or loveseat would do just fine!

Just strip off all of the upholstery from the furniture and add wooden slats for a seat and this sauna bench is ready to rock and roll! Now as for your heat source, let me give you a quick rundown as to how heating for a bathroom sauna can be accomplished. It's not at all complicated, and it can be fashioned together in basically about one day's time.

First, go to your local junkyard, snatch up an old gas can. I'm talking the old style, heavy duty metal canisters that the marines used to use! (Yep, this is hardcore!) Now take a grinder (or similar cutting tool) and slice right through the top of that can, cutting the head of the canister right off.

After you have done this get a metal bucket out, and then simply cut a hatch open and fit it to your canister. It should fit right on top without any trouble, but first you should sanitize it. Rinse and wash with soap and water before letting it soak in vinegar for a couple of hours. After cleaning out your newfound canister and metal bucket assembly take it into your bathroom and install it right in a corner away from anything that is flammable. You can now start putting your heating stones down into this canister assembly to warm your sauna. It's really as easy as that!

The Porta Potty Sauna

Ok, I realize that some of you may have been tempted to lose your lunch just from reading that sentence. But these portable toilet shacks that are so ubiquitous at construction sites and rock concerts can make for a readymade shell for a private sauna! You would take out the toilet and toilet tank before use of course, and have to sanitize it, but once this has been taken care of, the basic sealed off shell can serve as your sauna space!

The structure is already intact, complete with a sealable door. To get started, set out a foundation of cinderblocks for your porta potty. Place the porta potty down on this structure. Now you can work on the interior of the structure. First, add some 2 x 4's as braces for your benches, and attach hem to the wall. Next, take a sander and use it to round the 2 x 4's down at their ends.

Next get some floorboards for your floor of non permeable plywood and layer them down evenly at the floor of the porta potty. Now you just need a stainless steel bucket in which you can burn your hot stones so you can heat up your porta potty sauna! Invite the friend over and tell them that you've got something to show them. Because I can guarantee, as soon as they lay their eyes on this former potty shack turned sauna, they will be amazed!

Turn Your Shed into a Sauna

The structure of the common backyard shed makes for a perfect sauna, you just have to do some remodeling! And the first step in that remodeling is to get some R-grade insulation for the walls and ceiling. Try to use insulation with at least an R20 rating. Put down a couple layers of this stuff evenly on the walls and ceiling of your shed. Make sure that they are even so that no heat or steam will be able to seep out later on.

Next, you will need to place some foil over your layer of insulation in order to create what is known as a "moisture barrier" for your sauna. After you have put this in place you can then put up your plywood walls and flooring. Now just get out a durable metal container (such as an out of use propane tank) and set it in the center of the room so you can place your heating rocks inside and milk this fantastic sauna heat for what it is worth!

The Public Telephone Booth Sauna

This one is so darn weird, it just might work! The old styled telephone booths that used to be on every corner are now relegated to the junk yard. But if you happen to find one of these treasures from the past laying in the junk heap, don't pass it by, pick it up! This thing is a blast from the past, but to the junkyard owner, it is probably nothing more than junk just taking up space. But once you offer to take it off their hands, after shaking their heads in disbelief, they will probably thank you for taking it from them.

The telephone booth makes for an excellent sauna structure almost completely as is. All you really have to do is put in some R-grade insulation on the walls, and maybe some non permeable plywood on the floors. Find and old steel bucket to throw some coal in and this DIY alternative sauna is done! Now you can be just like superman diving into phone booths. But it doesn't take a superman to appreciate the power of this whimsical yet great design.

From Beater Van to Awesome Sauna

Yes, if you have an old van sitting in your driveway and you don't know what to do with it—why not turn it into a sauna? I have to admit, I actually did laugh when I heard about this one, but upon further investigation, it actually seems like a brilliant idea! The typical mini van has just enough space for the enterprise. So instead of letting the thing sit around and gather dust, rust, and cobwebs. Deck that baby out with the latest in sauna gear!

For construction, all you have to do is take out the seats and the rest of the upholstery since these would attract mold in the humidity, and begin the insulation process. You can use any type of R-grade insulation for this task; just make sure that it is strong. You can then use either tiles or plywood to seal up your floorboards. Next take out an old unusable propane canister and use it to heat up your stones. You will be driving in class and in comfort now my friends. You now have a mobile sauna!

Turn your Closet into a Sauna

Closet space can be easily and conveniently turned into a sauna. Just empty out anything already in the closet and then put some plywood down on the floor. Now add your insulation to the walls and add plywood to the walls as well. Put a small space heater in your closet and soon sauna styled heat will ensue. Just be very careful with this one, since most closets are a relatively small and cramped bit of space. Once these provisions have been taken into consideration however, there is no reason why you can't have your very own sauna right in the middle of your walk in closet! Just see what your spouse thinks about that!

Conclusion: Feeling the heat!

Saunas are a place of relaxation and healing. They have been used for thousands of years a place where the local people and culture can intermingle while stress and pain are melted away and evaporated with the heat. Many people in our high tech world of today have no idea what they are missing when it comes to such powerful holistic traditions.

Most inundate themselves with all of the latest gadgets and tech thinking that all of these artificial constructs will make them happy, and yet we are more stressed out than ever. But the profuse sweating produced by just a minute or so in the sauna can work away much of the anxiety that our artificial world has built up, as we increase circulation, blood flow, and oxygen in our bodies.

In today's world the very skin on our bones are neglected from unhealthy eating and sleep habits, but the sauna can rejuvenate that part of our life as well. The steam of the sauna can improve our skin's elasticity, texture, and over all tone. So next time you have the time, instead of buying a new smart phone, build yourself a sauna and feel that heat! Thank you for reading this book!

FREE Bonus Reminder

If you have not grabbed it yet, please go ahead and download your special bonus report *"DIY Projects. 13 Useful & Easy To Make DIY Projects To Save Money & Improve Your Home!"*
Simply Click the Button Below

OR Go to This Page
http://diyhomecraft.com/free

BONUS #2: More Free & Discounted Books or Products
Do you want to receive more Free/Discounted Books or Products?
We have a mailing list where we send out our new Books or Products when they go free or with a discount on Amazon. Click on the link below to sign up for Free & Discount Book & Product Promotions.
=> **Sign Up for Free & Discount Book & Product Promotions** <=

OR Go to this URL
http://bit.ly/1WBb1Ek

Printed in Great Britain
by Amazon